IMAGES
of America

HISTORIC HOTELS
OF LOS ANGELES
AND HOLLYWOOD

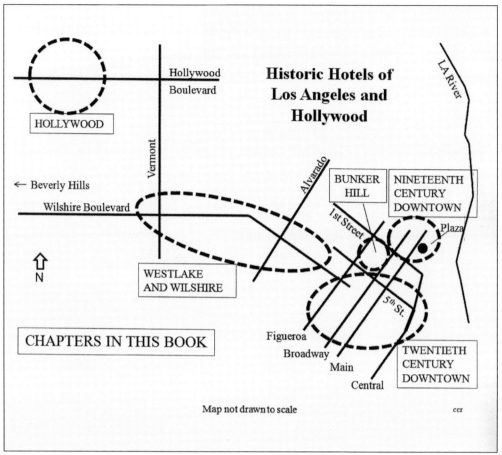

Historic Hotels of
Los Angeles and
Hollywood

LA River

Hollywood
Boulevard

HOLLYWOOD

Vermont

← Beverly Hills

Wilshire Boulevard

Alvarado

1st Street

BUNKER
HILL

NINETEENTH
CENTURY
DOWNTOWN

Plaza

⇑
N

WESTLAKE
AND WILSHIRE

5th St.

CHAPTERS IN THIS BOOK

Figueroa

Broadway

Main

TWENTIETH
CENTURY
DOWNTOWN

Central

Map not drawn to scale

ccr

This map provides a general outline of the geographic locations of hotels covered in this book.
(C. Roseman.)

IMAGES
of America

HISTORIC HOTELS
OF LOS ANGELES
AND HOLLYWOOD

Ruth Wallach, Linda McCann, Dace Taube,
Claude Zachary, and Curtis C. Roseman

ARCADIA
PUBLISHING

Published by Arcadia Publishing
Charleston, South Carolina

Printed in the United States of America

Library of Congress Control Number: 2008924122

For all general information, please contact Arcadia Publishing:
Telephone 843-853-2070
Fax 843-853-0044
E-mail sales@arcadiapublishing.com
For customer service and orders:
Toll-Free 1-888-313-2665

Visit us on the Internet at www.arcadiapublishing.com

CONTENTS

Acknowledgments   6

Introduction   7

1.   Nineteenth Century Downtown   9

2.   Bunker Hill   29

3.   Twentieth Century Downtown   49

4.   Westlake and Wilshire   81

5.   Hollywood   105

ACKNOWLEDGMENTS

The authors thank the following for their support and help: Carolyn Cole, Mathew Gainer, Giao Luong, Charles H. Matthews Jr., Matthew Mattson, Edwin McCann, Rick Mechtly, Andrew H. Nelson, Elizabeth M. Roseman, and John Taube.

The majority of images in this book were made available courtesy of the University of Southern California on behalf of the USC Libraries Special Collections. We drew mainly upon photographic archives held at the USC Regional History Collection (RHC). C. C. Pierce, a commercial photographer who documented the growth of Southern California from the late 19th century through the 1930s, created the California Historical Society/TICOR photographic collection (CHS). The *Los Angeles Examiner* photograph "morgue" is a collection of images that illustrate articles in the newspaper from the 1930s through the 1950s. The "Dick" Whittington collection was created by a commercial photographer whose studio was one of the eminent photography establishments in Southern California from the mid-1920s through the 1970s. The Community Redevelopment Agency Bunker Hill Archival Collection is composed of papers and photographs related to the Bunker Hill Redevelopment Project.

We also utilized images from the Security Pacific Collection at the Los Angeles Public Library (LAPL), which consists of 250,000 historic photographs of Los Angeles and Southern California covering the 20th century. Additional images came from the California State Library, the Miriam Matthews Charitable Trust, the California African American Museum, the Library of Congress, Marc Wanamaker/Bison Archives, and J. Eric Lynxwiler. We sincerely appreciate receiving permissions for use of the images from these various sources.

INTRODUCTION

Hotels have played distinctive roles in the development, function, and character of urban areas in the United States. Many hotel buildings have made a major impact on the visual landscape because of their size, orientation, location, signage or distinctive architecture. Hotels vary in their housing roles. Some host long-term residents and others primarily cater to short-term visitors. Hotels range from exclusive and expensive retreats for the wealthy, to basic no-frills shelter for those in need of low-cost temporary lodging or more permanent housing. Because they hosted major events or prominent people, or were the sites of disasters or tragedies, some hotels have become iconic symbols of the history of cities where they are located.

This book tells a history of Los Angeles and Hollywood by focusing on the great variety of hotels that have been part of the urban area from the 19th century to the 1950s. Hotels in the sprawling West Coast urban area have routinely provided lodging for tourists, business travelers, and residents. During the 20th century, presidents, international diplomats, leaders of industry, and movie stars visited Los Angeles in large numbers and stayed in the area's hotels. Los Angeles area hotels have hosted more nationally and internationally famous people than any other American urban area. Only New York may have surpassed Los Angeles in this regard.

We organized this book geographically (see the map on page 2). Each of the five chapters treats an important part of the Los Angeles urban fabric. We include Hollywood, which, in spite of its singular identity and perceived separateness, is actually located within the city of Los Angeles. The five regions were chosen because each has a distinct identity for its role in urban expansion and for the number, types, and ages of hotels that were located there in the past. We do not cover other parts of the urban area. Since before 1900, hotels have been established at a variety of locations across the sprawling urban area. In addition, important hotel clusters were established in beach communities including Santa Monica, and inland communities, such as Pasadena. These remain outside of the purview of this book.

We begin the first chapter by focusing on images of hotels in 19th-century downtown, an area that includes the original pueblo of Los Angeles that was settled in 1781. Today that original center of town is the site of the Los Angeles Pueblo Historic District. In the second half of the 19th century, as the pueblo grew to become a town and then a city, a major business district emerged that included numerous hotels.

Next we focus on Bunker Hill, a largely residential area just southwest of the original pueblo. In the late 19th century, wealthy Angelenos built large mansions on Bunker Hill, and by the turn of the century more modest homes and apartment buildings appeared alongside the opulent residences. Numerous small hotels, serving mainly residential clientele, were also built in the area.

These first two regions are distinctive because virtually all of the hotels built there are now gone, the Pico House being the lone exception. Government buildings gradually replaced commercial buildings in the 19th-century downtown as a very large Los Angeles Civic Center district emerged in that location in the 20th century. Bunker Hill was targeted for urban renewal in the 1950s, and within a couple of decades all of the hotel buildings, along with every other older building, had disappeared from the Hill. In their place today are tall office and residential buildings.

Our third region, represented by the longest chapter in the book, is the 20th-century downtown. From the middle to the end of the 19th century, Los Angeles grew from a village of a few thousand residents to a city of over 100,000. In the 1890s, the traditional business district near the plaza began expanding rapidly to the south and southwest, along major streets such as Main, Spring, Broadway, and Hill. A new 20th-century downtown was being created aside the older one. Much larger office and store buildings were built there, along with many hotels, most with modern facilities such as electricity and elevators. Some of the hotels were built on Main Street and east of Main to take advantage of proximity to railroad stations east of the downtown. But others, large and small, could be found mixed into the downtown urban fabric in most blocks. Today many of these hotel buildings remain in this area.

Our fourth region is Westlake and Wilshire. Near the turn of the century, hotels appeared on the outskirts of Los Angeles in the Westlake district, a growing area a few miles west of the center of town. Soon the city sprawled farther outward, especially with the increasing importance of automobile transportation. A major conduit of that sprawl was Wilshire Boulevard, along which major stores and institutions were being located, especially in the 1920s. Hotels, many of them upscale, also appeared along the boulevard and nearby parallel streets, expanding westward the hotel district in the Westlake area. Farther out Wilshire Boulevard, Beverly Hills also became home to high-class hotels.

Our final chapter treats the hotels of Hollywood. Hotels catering to tourists, especially winter visitors, were established Hollywood in the late 19th century. After Hollywood became part of Los Angeles in 1911, it experienced substantial growth owing to the rapidly expanding film industry. New hotels became an important part of Hollywood, hosting movie stars and other visitors, as well as cultural events, society dinners, and film industry events such as the Academy Awards.

One

NINETEENTH CENTURY DOWNTOWN

For most of the 19th century, Los Angeles was a small Western town. A decade after California was admitted into the United States in 1850, the town's population numbered fewer than 5,000. People of Mexican, Anglo, German, Italian, French, and African American descent constituted much of the population. Late in the century, after railroad connections were completed in the east, the population surged to more than 50,000 in 1890 and then doubled to 100,000 in 1900. While the early architecture of Los Angeles featured adobe-style homes, Victorian-style bungalows became popular during the end of the century. Residences stood close to the commercial areas. The rural parts were only several blocks away in any direction. The center included the old plaza and Commercial (now Alameda) and Main Streets. Late in the century, Anglo citizens became the majority, many becoming major investors in Los Angeles.

Whereas 19th-century Los Angeles had lodging houses, the Bella Union on Main Street was the first hotel. Early hotels were small and frequently changed ownership. They advertised a mix of American plans, which included meals, and European plans, which did not. The Pico House was known for modern conveniences such as bathtubs and gas lamps, and the Nadeau, the first four-story structure in the city, ushered in additional modern conveniences with its electric elevator, the first in the city. In the latter part of the century, the town's hotels, dining rooms, and saloons competed to be the swankiest. Nevertheless, they were known less for their quality, and more for the décor and for their customers and the personalities who owned and operated them. Most of the hotel buildings in the 19th-century downtown did not survive past the middle of the 20th century, and all are gone today. One by one, they disappeared as government buildings in the Civic Center took their place, while the downtown commercial district migrated to the south.

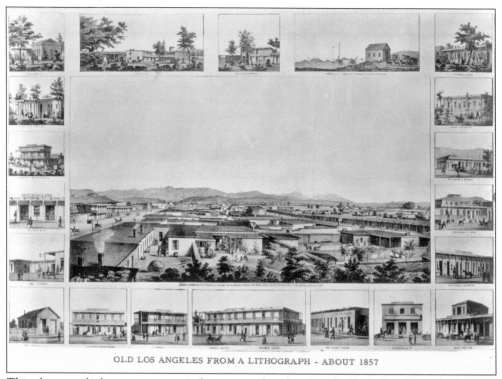

OLD LOS ANGELES FROM A LITHOGRAPH - ABOUT 1857

This photograph shows a panoramic drawing produced in 1857 by Kuchel and Dresel of Sonora Town. Among the businesses highlighted are the Bella Union (second from bottom left) and the Lafayette hotels (fourth from top right). Although there were earlier lodging houses, the Bella Union was considered the first hotel in the city. Charles Kuchel and Emile Dresel produced 50 lithographs of California townscapes between 1855 and 1859. (CHS.)

This view from the early 1870s shows the Bella Union Hotel at the 300 block of North Main Street, probably when Dr. James Brown Winston and Margarita Bandini Winston owned it. To the left of the hotel is the Farmers and Merchants Bank of Los Angeles. In 1873, the hotel changed names to The Clarendon, and around 1875 to St. Charles Hotel. (CHS.)

Veterans of the American War of 1812 are photographed in 1873 next to Bella Union. In the 1840s, a one-story adobe owned by Benjamin Davis Wilson stood here. It later became the last capitol of Mexican Alta California. The building served as quarters for American troops in the late 1840s, a saloon, a courthouse, and a commercial coach hub operated by Phineas Banning. In 1851, a second story was added, and a third in 1869. (CHS.)

Photograph of the St. Charles Hotel from the late 1870s shows several horse-drawn carriages parked along the curb. To the left of the St. Charles is the Farmers and Merchants Bank. A sign in the foreground reads, "Rifle and Pistol Shooting," a reminder that Los Angeles was a Western frontier town. (CHS.)

This view of the St. Charles Hotel was taken about 1926. The New Queen Restaurant occupied the ground floor. During the 1930s, the St. Charles turned into a low-budget-lodging house and served a poor and ethnically diverse population. It was demolished in 1940 to make space for a parking lot. In the 1970s, architect Robert Stockwell designed the subterranean Los Angeles Mall, where the oldest hotel once stood. (CHS.)

This undated photograph shows a drawing of Lafayette Hotel, built some time in the early 1850s. The second city hotel after the Bella Union (the U.S. Hotel was the third), it was renamed the Cosmopolitan Hotel and then became the St. Elmo. The Lafayette was located on Main Street near Temple, and in the 1870s was known as the best hotel in Los Angeles. (CHS.)

The Cosmopolitan Hotel can be viewed in the middle left of this 1875 pen drawing of Main Street, right above the Farmers and Merchants Bank. The Cosmopolitan was originally known as the Lafayette Hotel, and eventually became the St. Elmo. (CHS.)

This c. 1875 photograph shows the Lafayette Hotel stagecoach in an area of old Chinatown (currently Little Tokyo) known then as "Nigger Alley," an interpretation of the proper Spanish name "Calle de los Negros." This junction of Los Angeles, Arcadia, and Aliso Streets was also the location of the Chinese massacre of 1871. The low building in the background is the Coronel adobe that belonged to the family of Don Antonio Coronel, a prominent civic leader. (CHS.)

The St. Elmo Hotel, shown here about 1890, was located at the site of today's Los Angeles City Hall. In late 19th century, this area was a dense core of commercial and government buildings. During the first half of the 20th century, government buildings and plazas replaced most of the buildings, including the St. Elmo. (CHS.)

The U.S. Hotel was built around 1863 at 170 North Main by Louis Mesmer, then remodeled and expanded in 1886. The hotel attracted a swanky crowd and served the "best two-bit meal in Southern California" in its dining room, according to advertisements and articles published in the *Los Angeles Times*. By the early 1930s, it was still owned by the Mesmer family and lodged only men, many on public assistance. (CHS.)

Orpha Klinker is shown painting the U.S. Hotel in this photograph dated March 8, 1939. Later that month, the hotel was demolished. The painting was unveiled at a farewell dinner held in the hotel by the Los Angeles County Pioneer Society. Orpha Klinker (1892–1964) was a noted Southern California landscape painter. (LAPL.)

Shown here on March 25, 1939, are the remains of the U.S. Hotel during its demolition to make way for a more modern building. The *Herald Examiner* called it a "gaunt ghost of bygone gaiety of the early days of Los Angeles." (LAPL.)

Pico House Hotel, still standing near the Plaza, is pictured here about 1870. It was built in 1864 by Don Pio Pico, the last Mexican governor of California, and was considered the finest hotel in the West at that time, according to the *Los Angeles Times*. The hotel included bathtubs and gas lamps, an unusual luxury during those years. (CHS.)

The Old Fire House at 126 Plaza Street was designed by W. A. Boring in 1884. It was the second firehouse built by the city. Today it is the oldest standing firehouse in Los Angeles. In this *c.* 1920 photograph, Hotel Español occupied the second story, and the Cosmopolitan Saloon and the Locatuen Cigar Store were located below. (CHS.)

This *c.* 1874 photograph shows the early Plaza area seen northeast from Court House Hill. Behind First Congregational Church is the Kimball mansion; a lodging house on New High Street built that year by Myron Kimball and his wife. Helen Hunt Jackson stayed at the Kimball and worked on her novel *Ramona*. The mansion was replaced in the early 1900s by a federal building. (CHS.)

The first Los Angeles High School is being moved past the Clifton House, which is seen to the left of this 1888 photograph. Clifton House was the first brick hotel in Los Angeles. Thomas Pascoe built it in 1887 at Broadway and Second Streets. Thomas Pascoe came to Los Angeles in 1881 and operated several early hostelries, including the Kimball. He died in 1938. (CHS.)

This photograph taken in 1870 shows the White House Hotel at the far right on the southeast corner of Commercial (Alameda) and Los Angeles Streets. It was built about 1870 by John Schumacher, who obtained bricks from San Francisco and roofing tar from Hancock Park. The hotel was demolished and replaced by a parking lot in 1932. (CHS.)

This undated portrait shows Remi Nadeau (1819–1887), a French Canadian who arrived in Los Angeles in 1861. Nadeau's mule-and-wagon freight operations served miners in Inyo County. By 1873, he owned 80 teams. When he opened Hotel Nadeau in 1882, it was the first four-story structure in Los Angeles. (CHS.)

18

Remi Nadeau bought the plot on the southwest corner of First and Spring Streets in 1872 for $20,000. He opened Hotel Nadeau in 1882 with a grand ball attended by Southland's elite. The hotel installed the first electric elevator in Los Angeles. In this 1931 photograph, the Nadeau is seen across the lawn of Los Angeles City Hall, which was constructed in 1921. The hotel was demolished shortly after this picture was taken and replaced by the Los Angeles Times Building, which was designed in 1935 by Gordon B. Kaufmann in the Monumental Moderne style. (CHS.)

This is an undated drawing of the Pacific Hotel and the Passenger Eating Station, which adjoined the Southern Pacific Depot. Between 1876 and 1888, it was located north of the downtown area near the junction of the Los Angeles River and Arroyo Seco, in an area now called the "Cornfields." Its original proprietor, W. N. Monroe, was killed in a brawl at the railroad station in 1882. (LAPL.)

The Grand Central Hotel, which stood near the Bella Union at 326 North Main Street, was built in the 1870s and demolished in the early 1950s. In the early years it advertised weekly rates of $4 and meals for 25¢. Already by the time of this early 1890s photograph, the hotel's male boarders were occasionally known for drunken rows. (CHS.)

This mid-20th-century photograph shows various signs in front of the Grand Central Hotel, including an advertisement for transient-housekeeping rooms, as well as part of the signs for the Osaka Co. and a shoe repair. (LAPL.)

Hotel Westmoore at Seventh and Francisco Streets was photographed in 1910. Built around 1880, the 80-room, four-story frame structure was considered the finest family hotel in the Southland. It was among the first to have a ballroom and a banquet room. Its gardens stretched south to Eighth Street. By 1920, the Westmoore's reputation started to decline. (CHS.)

The Westmoore was torn down in 1957 to make room for a spacious garage and service station. Furniture and lumber from the hotel were sold in Tijuana at a public sale. In this 1957 photograph, a man points to the Statler Hotel, which was erected in 1952 at the corner of Figueroa and Seventh Streets. (Examiner.)

One of many hotels around Main Street, the Hotel Gray, shown in this c. 1905 photograph, was on the southern edge of the dense late-19th-century downtown, on the northeast corner of Third and Main Streets. Mrs. C. M. Gray built it in 1896. Mrs. Gray, who owned the hotel for more than a decade, regularly appeared in court for some business infraction or another. (CHS.)

Hollenbeck Hotel, built in 1884, is pictured here in 1905. It stood on the southwest corner of Second and Spring Streets and was demolished in 1931. When Elizabeth Hollenbeck and her husband opened the two-story hotel, the surrounding area was considered to be out in the country compared to the commercial center two blocks north at Court and First Streets. (CHS.)

The Natick House Hotel, photographed in 1939, opened in 1883 at First and Main Streets. The hotel had the first hand-operated elevator in the city. In 1899, John Parkinson refurbished it at the behest of its owner, the Bernard Estate. The Natick House was centrally located, opposite the opera house and near Los Angeles City Hall, and provided its guests a free bus service to and from all principal depots. (LAPL.)

Although streetcars were widely used for transportation around downtown in the late 19th and early 20th centuries, before the automobile came on the scene hotel guests were also treated to rides on special carriages. This 1910 photograph shows William Green, an African American driver of one of the carriage services serving downtown hotels in the 1890s into the early 1900s. (LAPL.)

This 1930s photograph shows Los Angeles City Hall, the Natick House Hotel, various storefronts, and the St. Louis Hotel in the foreground. Among the notables who stayed in the Natick House during its heyday were Theodore Roosevelt and Enrico Caruso. The Hart Brothers, noted Los Angeles hoteliers, owned the Natick for a while. The hotel was also popular with incendiaries and survived several arson attempts and a bomb wreck. (CHS.)

The Natick was razed for a parking lot in 1950, and its furnishings were sold at an auction. Here a superintendent of the wrecking crew points to murals on the walls of the old dining room at the hotel. The Natick dining room was popular and advertised its beautiful décor and competent waitresses. (Examiner.)

Hotel Florence, photographed here about 1905, stood at the southeast corner of Main and Third Streets. The business on its ground floor, Dean's Drug Store, was owned by Cameron E. Thom, who was city mayor from 1882 to 1884. Thom's house was behind the hotel. One of the signs in the store's window proclaimed, "For headache and exhaustion drink Coca-Cola, 5¢ a glass." (CHS.)

The Bellevue Terrace Hotel, pictured here in 1890, was a grand boardinghouse located on Figueroa and Sixth Streets. In 1892, Edward Doheny and his family stayed at this Victorian building. Doheny later said that he got the idea of digging for oil while watching wagons laden with fuel and tar pass by. In 1924, the Jonathan Club commissioned its Italian Renaissance building designed by Schultze and Weaver for this location. (CHS.)

The building pictured about 1890 was located on the southwest corner of Hope and Eighth Streets. D. W. Hanna constructed the building in 1887 for Los Angeles College, a boarding school for girls. It was bought in the 1890s by Abbot Kinney and operated as Abbotsford Inn and had 100 rooms. First Methodist Church purchased it in 1914 and demolished it in 1921 to build a new church building. (CHS.)

Hotel de Paris was on the second floor of the Jennette Block Building. The hotel is visible on the left of the photograph taken about 1925. The Jennette Block, constructed about 1888, was destroyed in the late 1940s for the construction of the Hollywood Freeway, which opened in December 1950. On the right, the Garnier Building is visible. The building was constructed in 1890 and is still standing at 415 North Los Angeles Street. (LAPL.)

The Ramona Hotel was located on the southwest corner of Spring and Third Streets from about 1890 into the early 1900s. Until about 1902, Tally's Phonograph and Bioscope Parlour was located on the ground floor next to the Ramona on Spring Street. In 1903 and again in 1912, architect John Parkinson was asked to design a new hotel for this location, which was never built. (LAPL.)

The Westminster Hotel, a large Victorian brick building with a six-story tower, is shown in this photograph taken about 1900. It was located at the northeast corner of Fourth and Main Streets. It was designed in 1887 by Robert B. Young and was considered the grandest hotel in the city. In about 1870, this area was the site of a Chinese market. By the mid-1930s, the hotel was in decline. The O. T. Johnson Corporation owned the Westminster until 1952. The Westminster is the only historic building to have been razed at the corner of Fourth and Main Streets (February 1960). Remaining today on the other three corners are the Barclay (Van Nuys) Hotel, the Farmers and Merchants Bank, and the San Fernando Building. (CHS.)

Two

BUNKER HILL

In the late 19th and early 20th centuries, Bunker Hill was marked by the rise of mansions with spires scattered among smaller and more modest edifices, including numerous hotels. By the late 20th century, office buildings and skyscrapers had replaced the original buildings on Bunker Hill.

Prudent Beaudry, a French Canadian who had arrived in Los Angeles in the mid-1860s, purchased a majority of Bunker Hill land and quickly turned it into profitable real estate. By the 1870s and 1880s, wealthy Angelenos built spacious Victorian mansions in Queen Anne and Eastlake styles, and by the turn of the century more modest homes, apartment buildings, and small hotels appeared alongside the opulent residences. New residents of Bunker Hill were professionals and businesspeople who commuted to the city below to work and shop. At the beginning of the 20th century, two incline railways, Angels Flight and Court Flight, connected the Hill with downtown. It efficiently served commuters, visitors, and tourists. By the 1920s, automobiles became popular in town, and Angelenos were moving outward at a rapid pace. Among those who migrated were the wealthy of Bunker Hill who left their palatial homes to be subdivided into rentals. Numerous hotels began serving elderly and low-income residents. Bunker Hill gradually became a depressed community.

After World War II, the deteriorating conditions of Bunker Hill prompted city and business leaders to develop an urban renewal plan. In 1960, the Los Angeles Community Redevelopment Agency announced the 136-acre, $315-million redevelopment project, which promised a modern acropolis of towering offices, hotels, and apartments. The *Los Angeles Examiner* reported it to be "the largest and most spectacular urban renewal program in the nation." In 1966, the first tower, a 42-story Union Bank Square, was completed as the tallest building in Los Angeles. By 1969, the only original buildings that remained on the hill were a home, two parking garages, the fire department headquarters, and three hotels.

In the 1880s, located one mile west of downtown Los Angeles, a scrubby hill transformed into an area of prime real estate development. Even before the hill had been named, the Second Street Cable line opened in 1885, carrying passengers from Second and Spring Streets over Bunker Hill, to the terminus at Second and Belmont. By the late 1880s, mansions and businesses owned by wealthy Angelenos such as the Witmer, Summers, and Lewis families, were dotting the hillside. Among the businesses were hotels, St. Paul's, the Huntley and the Belmont. The Belmont is visible in this 1886 view at the top of the hill. Surrounding the various edifices was manicured landscaping, a park, a lake and dancing platform. In 1889, a group of local citizens met to name the site Crown Hill. A few years later, in 1892, at the base of the hill at Second Street and Glendale Avenue, Edward Doheny and his partner Charles A. Canfield struck oil, an event that created a different type of boom and added another layer to Los Angeles history. (CHS.)

The Belmont Hotel on Crown Hill opened in July 1886 at the terminus of the Second Street Cable Railway that was completed a year earlier. The easy access to the line, the graceful architecture, beautiful landscaping, fresh air, and stunning views were attractions for visitors and wealthy Los Angelenos who held a number of social events there. The Belmont's owner, Rev. John W. Ellis, was also the proprietor and director of another Crown Hill establishment, Ellis Villa College, a finishing school for young ladies. (CHS.)

On December 16, 1887 about 10:00 a.m., a fire broke out in the tank-house of the Belmont Hotel. The hotel burned completely to the ground by noon. No person was seriously injured in the fire. Reports of rebuilding appeared in local newspapers the following few years, but no plans actually materialized. (CHS.)

This 1898 view shows Bunker Hill 30 years after Prudent Beaudry began to develop the 136-acre landmass that loomed over the city. Until then it was a barren landscape that sustained enough shrubbery and grasses for grazing sheep and cattle. Merchants, doctors and lawyers built Victorian mansions by 1870. During the next two decades apartment buildings and hotels popped up, including the Argyle, St. Angelo, Fremont and Trenton. During this period it was trendy to transform private residences into hotels. Two well-known examples are the Melrose and Richelieu. The recycling of homes into hotels or rooming houses heightened during 1920 and 1930 because wealthy people who lived downtown and Bunker Hill migrated to West Adams, the Park Avenue of the Los Angeles, and to Hollywood and Beverly Hills. Although some new hotels were built during the first few decades of the 20th century, there was little incentive to add new ones as tourists followed the westward movement. (CHS.)

Prudent Beaudry, a French Canadian and businessman, kindled the development of Bunker Hill in 1867, when he bought two adjoining plots of land at an auction for $517. He sold them a few years later for a substantial profit. Another successful venture was his Los Angeles City Water Company that supplied water to the hill. Beaudry served as mayor of Los Angeles from 1875 to 1876 and continued his pursuit of municipal improvements until his death in 1893. (RHC)

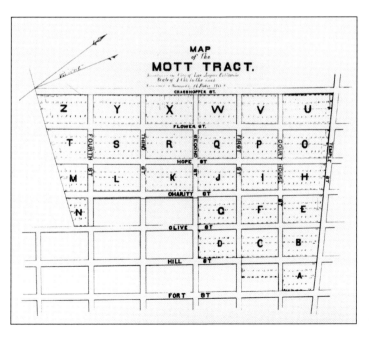

The Mott Tract map shows early Bunker Hill. George Hansen drew the map in 1868 for Stephen Mott, another successful developer in the area. He was also Prudent Beaudry's partner in the Los Angeles City Water Company. Some of the street names changed over the years. Grasshopper Street turned into Figueroa Street. Charity Street turned into Grand Street. Fort was renamed to Broadway, and the area surrounding Court Street became the Civic Center. (RHC)

The St. Angelo hotel at 237 North Grand Avenue was built during the boom of the 1880s when it was advertised as a European family-and-tourist rooming house. During the next few decades, the hotel and its guests were mentioned in the society pages. (CHS.)

The Second Street Cable was the earliest access line over Bunker Hill. In operation from 1885 to 1889, it ran from Spring Street to its western terminus at Belmont Avenue on Crown Hill. Andrew Hallidie constructed the line. He was the builder of San Francisco's famed cable line. This 1889 view shows a car making its way down Second Street at Broadway. (CHS.)

This 1900 photograph shows the northern end of Bunker Hill at the intersection of Broadway and Temple Streets. The four-story structure in the center belonged to the Women's Christian Temperance Union. The other buildings were residencies and boardinghouses. The ratio of boardinghouses to the amount of private homes continued to increase over the decades. (RHC.)

The Victorian three-story 30-unit Hotel Willoughby opened in 1898 was most likely owned by Mrs. E. Hollingsworth. By 1903, the hotel was operated by Ernest A. Pickering and Alice Brooks. Pickering was involved in a lawsuit by his wife over family support. In 1917, the Willoughby's furnishings were auctioned off, and the hotel closed. (CHS.)

As late-19th-century Bunker Hill kept pace with developing downtown Los Angeles, it became necessary to devise means for transportation between the two areas. Residents could carefully guide their carriages and buggies, and eventually their cars, up and down the steeply graded streets, which were paved by 1900. They could also ride the Second Street Cable line that operated from downtown, over Bunker Hill, to the terminus on Crown Hill. The Third Street Tunnel seen in this 1910 photograph was completed in 1900 and opened an east-west throughway between Hill and Hope streets. The Angels Flight incline railway, conceived and operated by Col. James Ward Eddy, provided quick access among the commercial establishments of downtown and the residences and hotels on the hill. When the railway was dedicated in 1901, Mayor Meredith P. Snyder and the women of the Olive Heights Association hosted a picnic for the town. The Hillcrest Hotel, positioned strategically near the top of the line, was built about 1904. (CHS.)

Pictured here in 1910, Occidental Hotel stood at 428 South Hill Street. In 1916, when purchased by hotelier A. Garrison von Ache, the building was a 170-room hotel. It was a hybrid of the Occidental and the former Broadway Hotel whose entrance was from Broadway Street. (CHS.)

The Munn Hotel at Fifth and Olive Streets is pictured here about 1900. It is one of the Bunker Hill hotels that have little historical documentation except for owner Arthur J Martin's legal difficulties. Nevertheless, it operated for several decades. In 1931, it was one of the official sites of the National Education Association conference. (CHS.)

This 1946 view shows three hotels known as "grand dames" of Grand Avenue between First and Second Streets. To the left is the Melrose annex, in the middle is the Old Melrose, and to the right the Richelieu. Both Victorian buildings were built as private residences in the 1880s. (CHS.)

Hotel Richelieu, seen here about 1956, was built in late 19th century. It was the home of Richard A. Larkin. In 1893, Mrs. Helen Larkin sold it to Chicago businessman Charles S. Hord who pledged to refurbish the building into a first-class hotel. The Richelieu was razed shortly before the Melrose in 1957. (LAPL.)

Mary Connor, daughter of Melrose Hotel owner Marc William Connor, is seated on a camel in front of the hotel during the Shriners' parade of 1906. That year, the parade was combined with the traditional and lavish annual La Fiesta de las Flores, a merging that was met with enthusiasm by the citizenry. When Presidents Theodore Roosevelt and William McKinley were in Los Angeles, they stayed at the Melrose. (Examiner.)

Mary Connor Rasche stands in front of the Hotel Melrose shortly before it was razed in May 1957. Its demise prompted Melrose resident and former opera singer Julia de Grazia Doerffel to write a passionate poem titled "Melrose Hotel. Good Bye!" It was discovered in the clippings morgue of the *Los Angeles Examiner*. There is no evidence that the newspaper ever published it. (Examiner.)

The Fremont hotel is pictured immediately after it was constructed in 1902 on the southwest corner of Fourth and Olive Streets. Architect John C. Austin designed and built it in the Mission style for well-known hotel developer Thomas Pascoe. By 1913, the hotel was in debt, and its then owner, the colorful Col. Richard A. von Falkenburg, was missing, possibly fleeing creditors. The hotel continued operating into the 1940s. (CHS.)

Two funicular railways, Angels Flight and Court Flight, served Bunker Hill. Visible in this 1946 photograph, Court Flight carried passengers from Broadway to Hill Streets at the northern end of Bunker Hill. An early, unfulfilled plan to attract tourists included the construction of two hotels near the top of the railway. The railway operated from 1904 to 1942 and was destroyed by fire two years later. (CHS.)

Hotel Rollin, located at the northwest corner of Third and Flower Streets and west of the Third Street Tunnel, is shown here in this photograph taken about 1905. Dr. D. W. Stewart sold the hotel to M. H. Taylor for $60,000 in 1905. The streetcar line provided easy access to other parts of the city, and the bakery on the ground floor attracted visitors and residents. (CHS.)

This photograph of the Trenton hotel at 427 South Olive Street was taken 1905. It was designed and built by architect Thornton Fitzhugh for Emma H. Peery at the cost of $90,000. Described as a European hotel, it contained 165 rooms, apartments, offices, and cafés. The hotel was noted for several of its modern features, such as telephones with long distance connections in each room. (CHS.)

Minnewaska was an unusual name in a city where buildings were generally baptized with English, Spanish, and French names. The name is of Dakota or Sioux origin and means "good water." Owner J. M. Shields guided the design and construction, which was completed in 1903. Despite its name, the building featured Mission-style details. Its spiral dome and lofty location established it as a Bunker Hill landmark. (California History Room, California State Library, Sacramento, California.)

By 1950, the still elegant Minnewaska served as a backdrop for several films, such as *Get out of Town*. Despite the sign, the hotel eventually met the same fate as its neighbors. In July 1964, a fire claimed three lives and badly damaged the building. In October, the wrecking ball completed its destruction as part of the Bunker Hill Urban Renewal project. (Examiner.)

Owner Fred E. Engstrum built the 220-room, six-story Engstrum Hotel at 623 Fifth Street. Its dedication in 1914 was reported as an evening of continual music and dancing without intermission. Residents of the hotel included film stars Charlie Chaplin and Rudolph Valentino. One of the last hotels to be razed as part of the redevelopment project, it was replaced by the 73-story Library Tower, the tallest structure west of the Mississippi. (LAPL.)

The 10-story Art Deco–style Monarch Hotel at Fifth and Figueroa Streets was designed and built in 1929 by architects Cramer and Wise. This 1958 photograph was taken to announce a major remodeling project, but by the mid-1960s, it was replaced by the 40-story Connecticut Life Insurance Company building. (Examiner.)

The 40-unit Ems Hotel at 321 South Olive Street near the top of Angels Flight railway was built around 1905 by contractor W. H. Griswold for the owner, Charles C. Emswiler. The image reveals the Mission-style architecture is a facade. Behind its front, is the continuation of a plain frame building. The California Plaza complex has replaced the Ems. (Community Redevelopment Agency of the City of Los Angeles.)

This late-1930s view shows the Hotel Moore Cliff complex gazing down on Hill Street as it tunnels underneath the northern end of Bunker Hill. When it opened in 1909, it was known as the Los Angeles Pacific Railway Tunnel and was hailed as a major thoroughfare to the undeveloped areas of Los Angeles and Hollywood. (Whittington.)

The 1955 panorama above reveals an area that was typical of Bunker Hill in its declining years. Residents were low-income wage earners, pensioners, artists, and writers, and none achieved the fame of earlier Hill writers Raymond Chandler and John Fante. The Stanley and other boxy rooming houses were prominent on the upper landscape, but a spire in the distance serves as a reminder that the elegant homes of the past had not all vanished. Figueroa Street was lined with a mix of modest residences and commercial establishments. The La Salle Hotel, seen in both views, gained fame when, in 1943, the *Los Angeles Examiner* reported that the district attorney filed a civil suit charging that unlawful acts were committed there. The gritty atmosphere of the Hill in the 1940s, 1950s, and 1960s provided the perfect backdrop for noir films such as *Criss Cross* (1949), *Kiss Me Deadly* (1956), and *Angel's Flight* (1965). (Community Redevelopment Agency, City of Los Angeles.)

The Grand Hotel at 416 South Grand Avenue was one of the many obscure establishments of Bunker Hill whose existence was recorded only in city directories. The above 1960 photograph shows the victim of a wrecking ball of the Bunker Hill Urban Renewal Project. The 1964 panorama below shows the Monarch Hotel at Fifth and Figueroa Streets waiting for destruction. It would be replaced by the Union Bank Square, which was completed in 1966. The nearby sea of parked cars was a familiar sight during the renewal project. The sites of razed building were replaced with parking lots, while development deals transpired and were finally forged, often after several years of negotiations. (Examiner and the Community Redevelopment Agency, City of Los Angeles.)

The 1959 petition for Angels Flight might have included a plea for all of Bunker Hill and its residents whom it served faithfully for 60 years. It continued to operate until 1969. Although within a few decades, it suffered a two-block relocation, a terrible accident, and cessation of its operation; it stands firm as an icon of Los Angeles and the single remaining link to historic Bunker Hill. (Examiner.)

In September 1961, the Hillcrest Hotel at 258 South Olive Street, adjacent to Angels Flight terminal, became one of the first victims of the demolition project ordered by the Community Redevelopment Agency as part of the Bunker Hill Urban Renewal Project. The CRA found new homes for its mostly elderly tenants who lived in the hotel for years. (Examiner.)

In 1959, the redevelopment plan for the Bunker Hill Project proposed displacement of 11,000 residents and demolition of all of its 396 buildings. Subsequent litigation delayed the process, but by the late 1960s the vision of a new Bunker Hill began to take shape. Most of the former buildings had been razed, and new structures were rising from the barren landscape. This 1968 aerial shows the white columned Dorothy Chandler Pavilion at the top center, which was part of the Music Center complex that completed in 1967. Landmark hotels Melrose and Richelieu used to stand one block southeast of the Music Center complex. The 42-story skyscraper is the Union Bank, which replaced the Monarch Hotel at Fifth and Figueroa Streets. Directly to the far right and partially hidden by the tower of the Los Angeles Public Library, stands the Engstrum Hotel, which was one of the last standing of the larger Bunker Hill hotels. Today the hill is home to several large hotels, office buildings, Walt Disney Concert Hall, the Cathedral of Our Lady of the Angels, and the Museum of Contemporary Art. (Whittington.)

Three

TWENTIETH CENTURY DOWNTOWN

In the early 20th century, Los Angeles expanded dramatically both in area and in population. Between 1900 and 1930, the city's population increased significantly from 100,000 to more than 1,000,000. By 1920, Los Angeles had more people than San Francisco. In the early 1900s, development had intensified as an attempt to make Los Angeles a commercial rival to San Francisco. Well-known architects designed businesses along Main, Spring, Broadway, Hill, and Olive Streets. The downtown commercial district moved south and west away from the 19th-century core near the plaza. With its large department stores and specialty shops, Broadway became the major shopping street. Spring Street, lined with bank buildings, became known as the "Wall Street of the West."

Several of the large early-20th-century downtown hotels were built along Main Street and close to the railroad stations east of downtown. Numerous smaller hotels were established east of Main, and other hotels, large and small, were scattered west of Main throughout the developing downtown area. Among the largest and most prominent downtown hotels in the 20th century were the Rosslyn on Main Street, the Alexandria on Spring Street, and the Biltmore on Pershing Square. Hotel developers and Los Angeles newspapers said each large hotel project was a rival of the St. Francis Hotel in San Francisco. Construction of downtown hotels was largely curtailed during the Depression and World War II. Then in 1950, the Statler opened on Figueroa Street, a precursor to a new hotel district that emerged on the western flank of downtown and close to the Los Angeles Convention Center and freeways. Although numerous pre-1930 downtown hotels were demolished after World War II, some still remain today. Included are both main-line hotels and others that serve low-income residents and transients.

This *c.* 1890s photograph shows the view facing north on Main Street from Fifth Street. In the foreground on the right is the Westminster, built in 1887, and in the distance on the right is the Gray. A dense commercial strip rapidly developed along South Main around the turn of the century and included hotels, theatres, restaurants, clubs, and other businesses. Later the Hotel Van Nuys displaced the grove of trees seen on the left. (CHS.)

The same area as above is seen here around 1924. The Victorian Westminster Hotel, demolished in 1960, is on the right. The Van Nuys, seen on the left, was constructed in the Beaux-Arts style, one of the first of a new generation of modern hotels built south of the old center of Los Angeles. It provided electricity and telephones for guests in every room. (CHS.)

The Van Nuys Hotel was designed in 1895 by Octavius Morgan and J. A. Walls in a Beaux-Arts style for Isaac Newton Van Nuys. This undated photograph shows the hotel's large rooftop sign, which lured customers from railroad stations to the east. Consolidated Hotels, Inc., leased the hotel in 1929, renamed it to Barclay, and renovated it to include a high-speed elevator and a remodeled lobby. (CHS.)

By 1970, the Barclay became home to pensioners and low-income families and suffered from several arson fires. The most notable happened in 1972. In 1983, this oldest still-operating hotel in Los Angeles was declared a Historic-Cultural monument. The stained glass on the ground floor diner might have been part of the renovations in 1935. The space once occupied by the diner is now used for filming. (R. Wallach.)

The Alexandria, which was designed in 1906 by John Parkinson, had 500 rooms and stood at the corner of Spring and Fifth Streets. Its proprietors were developers Robert Arnold Rowan and Albert C. Bilicke. Charlie Chaplin called the Alexandria the swankiest hotel in town, and United Artists film studio was formed here. Some believe a ghost of a grieving woman dressed in black haunts the hotel. (C. Roseman.)

Shown here around 1910 is the two-story lobby of the Alexandria, decorated with a large Christmas tree. The hotel's lobby was done in a Rococo style with marble columns and crystal chandeliers. Its Palm Court had a stained-glass ceiling. (CHS.)

The Mayflower Hotel, photographed in 2007, opened in 1927 at 535 South Grand Avenue. Charles F. Whittlesey designed the 12-story building in Spanish Moorish style for developer William H. Anderson. It had 348 rooms, each with a private bath. Room rates ranged from $2.50 to $7.50 per night. In the 1950s, it became part of the Hilton hotel chain and was renamed to Checkers Hotel in 1989. (R. Wallach.)

This photograph taken in 1880 shows a pen-and-ink drawing of the home of French Canadian pioneer Remi Nadeau that was located on the southwest corner of Fifth and Olive Streets. Two women play croquet in front of a simple clapboard cottage. On this site stands the Biltmore Hotel, which was built in 1923. (CHS.)

This *c.* 1920 photograph shows St. Paul's Pro-Cathedral at 535 South Olive Street. The church was built in 1883 and demolished in 1922 to make room for the Biltmore Hotel. The last service in the Cathedral was held on February 12, 1922. (CHS.)

The Biltmore Hotel, shown here in the 1930s, opened in 1923 and faced Pershing Square. Designed by Schultze and Weaver in a style combining Spanish and Italian architecture, it was built to accommodate 1,500 rooms, costing $10 million. When an addition opened in the 1980s, the hotel's main entrance shifted from Olive Street to Grand Avenue, so that it no longer faced Pershing Square and the historic core of downtown. (Whittington.)

Interior of the Biltmore Bowl, a 14,000-square-foot entertainment space, is pictured here in 1947. The Biltmore has other venues, such as the famed Crystal Ballroom (pictured below) where ceremonies of the Academy Awards were held eight times between 1931 and 1942. The hotel's 1,700-seat Biltmore Theater (no longer extant) was the city's premier venue for drama for many years. (Examiner.)

The Biltmore Crystal Ballroom, capable of seating 700 people, was photographed in preparation for the National Constitution Day ceremony in 1936. Its ceiling is the most elaborate of the artist Giovanni Smeraldi's work for the hotel. Mounted in its concave-domed surface is a single canvas of great proportion decorated with mythical figures. Two mammoth crystal lighting fixtures, imported from Europe, were suspended from the ceiling. (Examiner.)

This mid-1920s photograph shows one of 1,500 rooms at the Biltmore. Among the many people who stayed at the Biltmore were Franklin D. Roosevelt, John F. Kennedy, Jimmy Carter, and the Duke and Duchess of York. Over the years, the Biltmore also accommodated long-term residents, some who stayed for decades. (Examiner.)

This 1951 photograph is part of a series of houseware and jewelry shows that took place at the Biltmore. The model, Mil Patrick, is holding a large classically designed teaspoon with sterling tray and a bowl on the side. (Examiner.)

The Biltmore tower is pictured under construction in 1985. The renovation included the opening of the Grand Avenue lobby, formerly the music room and later the location of the headquarters for the 1960 Democratic National Convention. In the forefront are the First German United Methodist Church (opened in 1910) and the San Carlos Hotel, built about 1920 and housing the second Googie's Coffee Shop. Both were demolished in 1988 for the Gas Company Tower. (CHS.)

This c. 1897 photograph shows the John H. Jones residence on Main Street looking north from Fifth Street. This property later turned into the site of a series of Rosslyn Hotels. John H. Jones, born in Massachusetts, was a Los Angeles real estate pioneer who lived on this property during the late 1860s before moving to the West Adams area. Jones died in 1903. (CHS.)

The old Hotel Rosslyn at 433 South Main Street was previously called Hotel Lindsey. Abner Leonard Ross purchased it in 1898. By the time of this photograph in 1905, the hotel was owned by A. P. Johnson and operated by C. A. Harrison. Both were involved in the subsequent expansion of the Rosslyn into a much larger facility. (CHS.)

This 1904 view shows the Lexington Hotel on Main Street, abutting the south wall of the first Rosslyn Hotel on the right. In 1906 the Rosslyn expanded to include the six-story Lexington building. The result was a 280-room hotel. The Rosslyn would eventually build two larger structures just to the south (left) of the Lexington building. (CHS.)

The Security Trust and Savings Bank building is under construction on Spring Street at Fifth Street in this 1907 aerial photograph. The location of many financial banks, Spring Street was known as the "Wall Street of the West." The streetcar on Main Street, in the right foreground, would pass the front of the Rosslyn Hotel, which by this time included the former Lexington Hotel building. To the left of the bank building frame is the 500-room Alexandria Hotel. (CHS.)

Looking north on Main Street, this photograph taken in 1905 shows the first Rosslyn Hotel on the left and the Van Nuys in the middle. By this time, Main street was becoming a major hotel street. In the foreground is a trolley that connected the hotels on Main and neighboring streets with the Southern Pacific Arcade Depot some eight blocks to the east. (CHS.)

Built on the northwest corner of Main and Fifth Streets in 1914 by the Hart Brothers for $1 million, the 750-room new Rosslyn was rivaled on the West Coast only by San Francisco's St. Francis. In 1923, the Rosslyn Annex opened and replaced a commercial building that stood on the plot owned by the Edwards family since 1868. The revamped Rosslyn was the largest hotel on the Pacific Coast with 1,100 rooms and 800 baths. The hotel's two parts were connected by two subways that ran under Fifth Street. One was used by guests, and the other was reserved for staff. Both buildings were designed by the Parkinson firm in Italian Renaissance style. The L went into decline and closed in 1959. It reopened in 1979 as two hotels, the Rosslyn on the south side, and the Frontier on the north side. (CHS and the Examiner.)

This photograph from October 10, 1951, shows the dead body of George Miller, a Barstow railroad laborer, after a fight at a bar on the ground floor of the Rosslyn. The photograph's caption in the *Los Angeles Times* said, "His body lies covered on the floor with bar patrons evidencing little concern, only two bothering to gaze at the victim." (Examiner.)

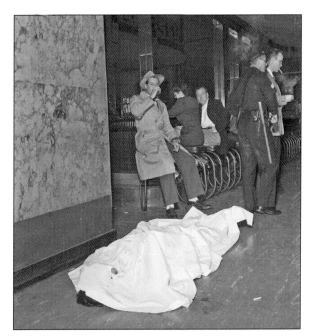

King Edward Hotel, located on Fifth and Los Angeles Streets, was designed by Parkinson and Bergstrom in 1906 with 150 rooms and operated on the European plan. Pictured here in 2007, it was considered a handsome hostelry with good access to the railroad depots, where tourists arrived. In its earliest years, the King Edward was operated by Col. Edward Dunham, who also operated the Nadeau Hotel. (R. Wallach.)

Hotel El Rey, pictured on a 1930s postcard, was located at Fifth and San Pedro Streets. Built in 1926 with 621 rooms, it became one of the largest among a number of smaller hotels located between Main Street and railroad depots to the east. In 1981, the El Rey became home to the Weingart Center Association, which still provides shelter and various social services to more than 600 homeless men and women at this skid row location. (C. Roseman.)

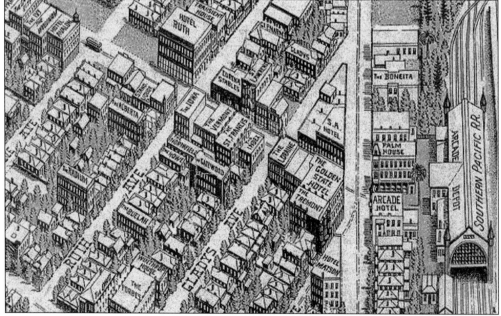

By the early 20th century, dozens of smaller hostelries lined Fifth Street between the downtown core and the Southern Pacific Arcade Depot on Central Avenue. This 1909 panoramic map shows some of the hotels and the depot, which was built in 1888 and replaced in 1914 by Central Station. (Library of Congress.)

This 1978 night scene shows two hotels, the Harold and Panama, along Fifth Street at San Julian Street. Through the last decades of the 20th century, this area became part of Skid Row and most of the hotels lining Fifth Street became single-room-only facilities for the periodic homeless. In 1985, the non-profit Single Room Occupancy Housing Corporation renovated the 250-room Panama. (LAPL.)

On July 30, 1955, Susan Hayward and her entourage visited the Delux Hotel on Fifth Street in Skid Row to film *I'll Cry Tomorrow*. In the movie, Hayward played the part of Lillian Roth, who suffered from and eventually conquered alcoholism. Hayward won an Academy Award nomination for the role. The film also featured Richard Conte, Eddie Albert, Jo Van Fleet, and Don Taylor. (LAPL.)

This undated photograph shows the exterior of the original Hotel Baltimore. Built in 1896, it stood at Seventh and Olive Streets and was owned by mining magnate John Brockman. The hotel was purchased by the Los Angeles Athletic Club for $450,000 in 1907 and was demolished for the construction of the club's headquarters. (LAPL.)

The "new" Hotel Baltimore still stands on the southwest corner of Fifth and Los Angeles Streets. Although it is one block east of Main Street, the lure of a Main Street address led the hotel to describe its location with reference to Main Street in this 1920s postcard. The 215-room hotel was built in 1910 by Thomas Ashton Fry and designed by architect Arthur Rolland Kelly. (C. Roseman.)

Ralphs grocery stores and supermarkets have a long history in Los Angeles. This 1886 photograph shows the first Ralphs Bros. Grocers store at the southwest corner of Sixth and Spring Streets. Included in the picture are brothers George A. Ralphs and Walter B. Ralphs. Twenty years later, the Hayward Hotel replaced the market on this corner. (LAPL.)

Charles F. Whittlesey designed the Hayward Hotel at Sixth and Spring Streets in 1906 for Harris C. Fryman. In 1925, architects John and Donald Parkinson designed two additions on either side of the original corner building. In 2004, the Living Urban Museum of Electric and Neon Signs project restored and relit the large vertical neon Hayward sign, which was installed on the building a few years after this photograph was taken in 1927. (CHS.)

This 1905 photograph shows the Angelus Hotel, located on the southwest corner of Fourth and Spring Streets, one block west of Main. The Angelus, with 200 rooms, was opened in 1901 by Gustavus S. Holmes. In 1924, it served as headquarters for Republican Party presidential candidate Calvin Coolidge. The Angelus was razed in 1956 and replaced by a parking lot. (CHS.)

Hotel Cecil is shown in the foreground in this mid-1920s photograph. The headquarters of the Pacific Electric Railway Company and hub of the interurban Red Cars is also visible. Robert H. Schops opened the Cecil in 1924 at 640 South Main Street. The Barker Brothers firm furnished the hotel's 700 rooms. Similar to many hotels around Main Street, it became mostly a residential hotel after World War II. (LAPL.)

This 1935 photograph of a woman on a flagpole was taken near Eighth and Spring Streets. Hotel Cecil on Main Street is visible in the background. Hotel Jovita and its annex extended a full block from Spring to Main Streets and are visible in the front of the photograph. (LAPL.)

This 1920s photograph shows Hotel California nestled among various retail stores on Broadway Street at Fifth Street. Broadway was the main shopping street in downtown Los Angeles for most of the 20th century. The large building in the center housed the Broadway Department Store. (LAPL.)

This 1907 photograph shows the Hotel Lankershim, which was designed by Robert B. Young at Seventh and Broadway Streets. The hotel opened in 1905 with 250 rooms and 160 baths. Col. J. B. Lankershim, son of Bavarian-born landowner Isaac Lankershim, owned the building. Before the Rosslyn, Hotel Lankershim was supposed to have rivaled the St. Francis in San Francisco. (CHS.)

This photograph taken in 1900 shows the interior of the Lankershim, which included two large landscape paintings on the walls, illuminated by chandeliers. By the mid-20th century, the hotel lost its luster. (CHS.)

In 1900, H. C. Eagon opened the Portsmouth Hotel, which was located at 512–522 Hill Street. Dawson's bookstore operated on the first floor of the building in the second decade of the 20th century. It was a prime location because it faced Central Park, known today as Pershing Square. Portsmouth was photographed here in 1951 after Eastern investors acquired it from Alice Larkin Toulmin for $750,000. Although the new investors planned to improve it, the hotel closely shortly thereafter. (Examiner.)

This 1932 photograph shows two hotels on Hill Street, the Portsmouth in the foreground, and the Clark to the far left. Banners celebrated the arrival of the Olympic Games, the first of two Olympiads to be hosted in Los Angeles (the second in 1984). Designed by architect Harrison Albright in 1912, the Clark Hotel opened with 555 rooms. (LAPL.)

Hotel Ritz, at 813 South Flower, is shown here after being renovated in 1930. The front of the building was set back five feet because the street was widened, and the fire escape was set inside. The hotel's exterior was cleaned. It is now known as the Ritz Milner and is part of a national chain of hotels started in 1918 by Earle R. Milner. (Examiner.)

Stanton, Reed and Hibbard erected Figueroa Hotel in 1926 for the YWCA at 939 South Figueroa Street. The project cost more than $1 million to build. The 409-room Figueroa Hotel was considered the largest project of its kind to be built, financed, owned, and operated by women. Nine floors were reserved for women and two for men with families. Late in the 20th century, the hotel, photographed in 2007, was restored and redecorated with a Moroccan motif. (R. Wallach.)

Hotel Savoy, erected in 1920 and photographed here in 1933, stood at Sixth and Grand Streets. Frank Simpson Sr. owned the property, and his son operated the hotel. Architects Morgan, Walls and Clements designed the building. All the rooms included private baths, and the hotel was considered to be one of the finer hostelries in the city. It was demolished in 1965. (CHS.)

This 1940 billboard, located along the railroad tracks about seven miles from downtown Los Angeles, advertised the Savoy Hotel to potential customers. Before World War II, the majority of patrons of most downtown hotels arrived in Los Angeles by train. (LAPL.)

The Bristol Hotel opened in 1927 at 423 West Eighth Street and had 150 rooms. Photographed here in 1953, it served a low-income population and closed in 2004 for a pending renovation and a remake into an upscale 80-to-100-room hotel for a high-end clientele, with a rooftop bar, a nightclub in the basement, a restaurant, and an exclusive movie theatre for guests. (Examiner.)

Embassy Hotel and Auditorium, shown here in the second decade of the 20th century, is located at 849 South Grand. Thornton Fitzhugh and Frank G. Krucker designed the Italian Renaissance–style hotel in 1914 for Trinity Methodist Episcopal Church. South. Its 325 residential rooms were designed to be used by men. The building also included office space and a theater. It was also a site for musical performances and religious and political meetings. (CHS.)

The Stillwell Hotel at 838 South Grand Street, is shown here in the second decade of the 20th century. Noonan and Kysor designed it in 1912 for real estate owner Charles H. Stillwell. When the Stillwell hotel was renovated in the 1950s, many of its decorative elements were removed. In 1987, owner T. S. Gill restored the hotel to its former glory and upgraded its 250 rooms. (CHS.)

Hank's Bar and American Grill was opened by retired professional prizefighter Henry "Hank" Holzer on the ground floor of the Stillwell in the 1950s. The restaurant is noted for its wood-paneled walls and red velvet decor. Among the bar's permanent denizens is Lady Greensleeves, photographed with an admirer in 2006. (R. Wallach.)

Dr. John Alexander Somerville, pictured here in 1953, built the elegant Somerville Hotel in 1928 with his wife, Dr. Vada Jetmore Somerville. John Somerville was the first African American graduate of the School of Dentistry at the University of Southern California in 1907. Vada Somerville graduated from the School in 1918. The Somervilles founded the Los Angeles chapter of the NAACP in 1914 and continued to be prominent community leaders. (Examiner.)

The Somerville hotel at 4225 South Central Avenue, photographed in 1928, was the first hotel in this country that was opened specifically for African Americans. Lucius Lomax purchased it after the 1929 stock market crash and renamed it Dunbar, after the poet Paul Laurence Dunbar. The upstairs nightclub became a hotbed of jazz entertainment, for which Central Avenue was nationally known. In 1974, the hotel was declared a Los Angeles Historical-Cultural Monument. (The Miriam Matthews Charitable Trust.)

Hotel Darby at 234 West Adams Street is shown here in 1925. John C. Austin designed it in 1909 for landowner Wesley Clark in French Renaissance style. It was constructed of reinforced concrete, brick, and steel. The Darby was an apartment hotel containing 70 bathrooms, and 130 rooms with built-in wardrobes, which was considered a novel luxury. It changed its name to Grace in the 1940s and was purchased by the United House of Prayer church after World War II. (Whittington.)

This undated photograph taken in front of Hotel Darby shows Charles S. Blodgett, a prominent African American building contractor seated in the front of the car. The photograph identifies him as the builder of the Darby. Blodgett was the brother of Louis M. Blodgett, who was president of the Liberty Savings and Loan Association. (LAPL.)

Pictured here c. 1918 is the Foy residence, which stood on the northwest corner of Figueroa and Seventh Streets and later became the location of the Statler Hotel. In the 1920s, the Foy residence displaced the Arnold building, which housed the Hudson and Essex motorcars. By the 1930s, Paul G. Hoffman Co. Inc. Studebaker car dealership stood north of the building. (CHS.)

This photograph from the 1880s shows Mary E. Foy standing against a painted backdrop, which was typical of a photographer's studio. Foy was the city's first full-time salaried librarian, from 1880 to 1884. Involved in civic affairs throughout her life, she also ran for state congress in 1934. (LAPL.)

The ground-breaking ceremony for the Statler Hotel at Figueroa and Seventh Streets was held on July 6, 1950. This photograph shows California governor Earl Warren at the controls of the steam shovel, standing next to actress Celeste Holm. From left to right are Statler vice president Howard Dugan, Los Angeles mayor Fletcher Bowron, Statler vice president H. B. Callis, Statler board chairman William Marcy, and Statler company head Arthur Douglas. (Examiner.)

The Statler, billed as the largest hotel in Los Angeles, is shown here in 1952. It was designed as a luxury hotel with 1275 rooms, 500-car garage, a laundry facility capable of serving a city of 20,000, and 70,000 square feet of shops. By 1950, the downtown's retail sector had extended westward along Seventh Street and private automobile travel had supplanted rail, so this location made sense for a new hotel. (Whittington.)

A unique feature of the Statler was a motorist's lobby for guests who arrived by car. The hotel's publicity stated, "The motorist can drive his car into the lobby, turn it over to an attendant for parking in the underground garage and go directly to his room without the need of going to the main lobby in travel-wrinkled clothes." (Examiner.)

The Statler's Terrace Room is pictured on opening night in 1952. The stage was hydraulically controlled and could be lowered to slide under the band dais to expose the ice rink used for skating acts. (Examiner.)

On October 31, 1952, shortly after the hotel's official dedication, 200 maids at the Statler were presented with orchids "for providing immeasurable comfort to guests." Philip Corrin, Bullock's Downtown general manager, and Delia Cooper, executive housekeeper of the hotel presented the flowers. (Examiner.)

The main Statler kitchen, shown here in 1952, was one of the largest in the world. In addition to this kitchen, the Statler had another kitchen to take care of the needs of the ballroom patrons and a third kitchen located at the employees' cafeteria. The Statler kitchens could jointly prepare meals for 15,000 people in one day. (Examiner.)

This promotional photograph from 1952 says guests can enjoy "a typical guest room, studio type, at the Los Angeles Statler. All rooms in the hotel are air-conditioned, have television, radio and wide picture windows. Beds are couches in the daytime to give a living-room affect. All fixtures are tailor-made to fit the rooms." (Examiner.)

This promotional photograph shows view of "a typical Statler bathroom. The washbowl shelf is extended to provide a working service for the convenience of guests using the large mirror. Lighting is indirect fluorescent. All bathroom fixtures were especially designed for this hotel." (Examiner.)

Four

WESTLAKE AND WILSHIRE

Wilshire Boulevard, the grandest commercial avenue in Los Angeles, roughly follows the route originally set by Native American paths and explorers' trails 16 miles westward from downtown Los Angeles to the Pacific Ocean. The development of this imposing thoroughfare was very piecemeal. In 1895, real estate speculator H. Gaylord Wilshire gave his name to a main street of 1,200 feet in his new subdivision directly west of Westlake Park (named in 1890) and east of Hoover Street on the outer fringes of the original pueblo boundaries. In 1885, Orange Street had developed from the eastward edge of Westlake Park to the center of downtown. In order to widen the street and improve the growing traffic congestion, it was renamed Wilshire Boulevard in 1924. The Wilshire Center and Miracle Mile section, from Hoover west to Fairfax Avenue, was completed in 1927, and the final link was built in late 1934, when a causeway cut through Westlake Park completing the connection of the Boulevard from downtown to Santa Monica.

No streetcar line was built down Wilshire Boulevard's length. Initially the Gaylord Wilshire development was a residential enclave for the wealthy, including Harrison Gray Otis, the owner of the *Los Angeles Times*. Due to increasing property values, exclusive hotel and apartment complexes were built around Westlake Park beginning at the turn of the century, starting with the Hershey Arms Hotel (1902), the Hotel Leighton (1904) north of Westlake on Sixth Street, the Alvarado Hotel (1902), and Hotel Pepper (1904). The hotel district grew slowly and extended westward with hotel apartments such as the Bryson (1913), until the Ambassador Hotel opened in 1921 and initiated a spurt of building for the rest of the decade along the boulevard. This district, associated with the Westlake area, terminated at Normandie Avenue to the west. Commercial buildings, exclusive residential communities such as Fremont Place and Hancock Park, and the Miracle Mile covered the area between Normandie and the city of Beverly Hills. Beverly Hills had its first Wilshire Boulevard hostelry open in 1928, and the Beverly Hilton marked the eastern boundary of that city in 1955.

One of the earliest hostelries west of downtown was the Mondonville Hotel on Washington Boulevard near Arlington Road, photographed c. 1896. The hotel was renamed the Army and Navy Clubhouse. Mondonville was a development of 287 lots owned by C. Mondon, fronting on Adams and Washington Streets, that opened in 1887. The hotel developed a rather unsavory reputation and was put out of business in 1903. (CHS.)

The Hotel St. Paul, 1021 West Sixth Street at St. Paul Place, opened in 1927 and was designed by architect John V. Koester. The Hotel had 10 stories with 150 rooms and sported a modified Spanish design with a terra cotta and fancy brick exterior. The interior spaces were finished in Philippine mahogany and walnut. The dining room was staffed with a European maître d'hôtel and a Swiss chef. (RHC.)

The Mayfair Hotel, 1256 West Seventh Street at Hartford Avenue, also opened in 1927. It was designed by Alexander E. Curlett and Claud W. Beelman with 13 stories and 350 rooms, and was built for $1,500,00. Its Rainbow Isle Room featured dining and dancing with the Rainbow Isle Orchestra, broadcast over radio station KFWB every evening. It was renovated in 1985. (Whittington.)

Hotel Pepper, photographed in 1905, opened in February 1904 on the corner of Seventh Street and Burlington Avenue and was designed by C. H. Brinkhoff in Spanish Renaissance and Moorish architecture. It had six stories, an observation tower with eight stories, and approximately 100 rooms. Most of the rooms had a private bath, which was a luxury at the time. It was named in recognition of the previous owner of the land upon which it was built. (CHS.)

Hotel Alvarado (2065 West Sixth Street at Alvarado) was built in 1903 by William B. Corwin for $50,000 and designed by John C. Austin as one of the first sizable improvements in the Westlake District. The three-story, 100-room Spanish Renaissance–style building had Mission features, including turrets on two corners. The grand dining hall seated 250 and overlooked Westlake Park. The roof garden had an expansive city view. Theodore Roosevelt and William Howard Taft were both guests. (CHS.)

Hotel Leighton (2127 West Sixth Street) was designed by John C. Austin and built by George A Leighton in 1904. It originally had 104 rooms but was expanded in 1912 to include the entire block between Alvarado and Lake Streets. Many Southern California Tennis Club tournaments were played on its tennis courts during World War I. (CHS.)

This photograph shows Lake View Hotel, located at 2215 West Sixth Street, overlooking Westlake Park. The three-story hotel, built in 1908, contained 55 rooms. (CHS.)

The 220-room William Penn Hotel was built in 1927 at the end of the development boom in the mid-1920s at 2208 West Eighth Street at Lake street on the south side of Westlake Park across from the Lake View. It featured a cocktail lounge, dining room, coffee shop, and several gardens. The Pepperdine Foundation owned it in the 1930s and 1940s. (Whittington.)

This bird's-eye view looking east down Wilshire Boulevard shows Westlake Park in the foreground and the Lake View Hotel and Hotel Leighton on the left. (Whittington.)

This photograph shows a bird's-eye view looking west down Wilshire Boulevard. Westlake Park is in the foreground. From right to left are the Asbury Hotel, Elks Lodge 99, Arcady Hotel, Park Wilshire Hotel, Lafayette Park, and the Town House beyond. (Whittington.)

The Lodge 99 of the Order of Elks Building, located at 607 South Park View Street, was designed by Curlett and Beelman and built in 1925 and 1926. It was sold in 1966 and renamed Park Plaza Hotel. Seen here in 1930, the Beaux-Arts, etched-concrete structure is half mastaba, or squared-off Egyptian pyramid, and half nine-story hotel with 160 rooms that rise out of the mastaba. A pair of crystalline plinths rises to become molded architectural warrior angels at each face of every corner, which are topped by a squashed urn. The hotel also has angels that are about twice as high as the others, guarding plinths along each side. The brilliant Art Deco interior of the hotel is a popular site for filming, weddings, and parties. The Art Deco design is apparent in the oversized stairway, the murals by Anthony Heinsbergen, the vaulted ceilings in the lobby, and the three ballroom-type halls. (Examiner.)

The Asbury Hotel Apartments at 2501 West Sixth Street at Carondelet were designed by Norman Alpaugh and built by E. A. Wayt in 1925 and included 94 apartments. According to newspaper reports, the structure represented "the limit of modern achievement in apartment-house construction," with full electric heat and electric stoves in each kitchen. (Whittington.)

The Victoria Arms Hotel Apartments, designed by Russell and Alpaugh, was located at 2424 Wilshire Boulevard between Park View and Carondelet Streets, and opened in 1924. It had eight stories including 134 two-room apartments, 36 three-room apartments, and two five-room suites. It departed from the prevalent Mediterranean and Craftsman variants of the era with its elegant, functional style and brick facing, which influenced the design of later buildings in the neighborhood. (Examiner.)

Victoria Arms was sold and renamed Park Wilshire in early 1930s. It was patronized by Robert F. Kennedy and other notables and was renovated in 1982. It is seen here near Westlake Park with the Shoreham Hotel to the south. (Whittington.)

George W. Kitchen built the Shoreham Hotel, located at 666 Carondelet Street south of Wilshire, in 1911. Its four-story Mission-style structure held 100 rooms and was styled as a residence or family hotel. (CHS.)

The Hershey Arms Hotel at 2600 Wilshire Boulevard was the first hotel built on Wilshire. The English Renaissance brick structure designed by John C. Austin covered the entire block between Rampart Boulevard and Coronado Street on the south side of Wilshire. Opened in 1902 by Mira Hershey, a wealthy Iowan spinster who also owned the Hotel Hollywood, it was home to many international celebrities and the rendezvous of local society for more than 30 years. With its garden and exotic furnishings, it was one of the landmarks of early-20th-century Los Angeles. It was demolished in 1956 and replaced by an office building for Western and Southern Life Insurance Company. (J. Eric Lynxwiler.)

J. B. Lilly and Paul Fletcher built the Arcady Apartment Hotel at 2619 Wilshire at Rampart for $2,250,000 in 1927. Designed by Albert R. Walker and Percy A. Eisen, it had 12 floors and 396 guest rooms that were divided between two, three and four-room suites. The Arcady turned into a retirement hotel in 1953, then into the Wilshire Royale Hotel, and was subsequently bought by Howard Johnson in 1986. (Marc Wanamaker/Bison Archives.)

The Bryson Apartments at 2701 Wilshire at Rampart is a 10-story Beaux-Arts, Classical Revival, and Mediterranean-style building designed by Frederick Noonan and Charles H. Kysor. It opened on January 10, 1913, and is named for its builder, Hugh W. Bryson. It was featured in Raymond Chandler's novel *The Lady in the Lake* and was owned for a time by actor Fred MacMurray. (CHS.)

A view of Wilshire Boulevard looking west at Lafayette Park shows the Town House hotel, also known as Sheraton Town House, on the right, and Bullock's Wilshire department store on the left. The Gaylord Apartments are seen in the central distance. (Whittington.)

Photographed above in 1955, the Town House, at 2961 Wilshire, is a Beaux-Arts-style, 300-room, 13-story, red brick and cast stone building designed by Norman Alpaugh. It was opened in 1929 at a cost of $4 million as an apartment-hotel overlooking Lafayette Park. It relaunched in 1937 as a luxury hotel and had a first-floor supper club named the Zebra Room, pictured below in 1955. Conrad Hilton took over in 1942, and then the Sheraton Hotels Corporation ran the hotel from 1958 until it closed in 1993. It was converted to low-income family apartments and reopened in 2001. (Examiner.)

This view looking east down Wilshire Boulevard from Shatto Street shows the Asbury and Arcady Hotels in the central distance, which are flanked by the Town House on the left and Bullock's Wilshire on the right. (Whittington.)

The Park Lane Apartment Hotel, located at New Hampshire and Fourth streets, opened in February 1927. Photographed in 1929, it was designed by Leland A. Bryant (most famous for the Art Deco Sunset Tower Apartments in West Hollywood) in Spanish Renaissance style, with a floral patio containing a "wealth of tropical vegetation, including banana, bamboo and date palms," as reported in the *Herald Examiner*, and a Spanish wishing-well. (Examiner.)

Curlett and Beelman designed the Talmadge Apartments located at 3278 Wilshire Boulevard. Photographed here in 1952, it opened in 1924, and was home to society and business leaders, and entertainment figures, such as Norma Talmadge, for whom it was named, and her husband, Joseph Schenck. (Examiner.)

The Windsor Apartments at 3198 West Seventh Street at Catalina opened in March of 1927 as one of the largest and most elegant apartments in Los Angeles. The English Tudor apartments were built and owned by Samuel Rabinowitch. Serving both as an apartment building and hotel, the Windsor was known as a place where Jews could stay without facing the prevalent discrimination of the time. It also featured excellent restaurants. (Examiner.)

The Ambassador Hotel was located at 3400 Wilshire Boulevard between Catalina and Mariposa. It was the first grand resort hotel in Los Angeles and moved the city's center of gravity westward, which helped establish Wilshire as the extended Main Street of Los Angeles. From its opening day on January 1, 1921, the hotel was successful. It was a tourist attraction, a fashionable winter residence, and a prominent social center. The sprawling central building and surrounding smaller bungalows were designed by Myron Hunt in the style of salmon-colored Italian villas. The 23-acre grounds were filled with lawns and flowers. Gardens along the side and in the rear contained pergolas, putting greens, fountains, tennis courts, health club, wooden jogging track, and a swimming pool with its own sandy beach. Inside the main building were stylish shops, a movie theatre, and the Cocoanut Grove nightclub. This photograph was taken during a performance by the Andrews Sisters in 1952. (Whittington.)

The Ambassador featured a large outdoor rectangular pool and a small circular pool for children, which were both designed by Walker and Eisen. Diving equipment and dressing rooms were available for guests. (CHS.)

The ascendancy of the automobile on Wilshire Boulevard was acknowledged by the ample parking space offered at the Ambassador to accommodate the vehicles of its upscale clientele. (CHS.)

The Ambassador had an 18-hole miniature golf course on its eastern and southern lawn, the site of many pitch-and-putt tournaments. Water golf and golf croquet were also popular entertainments at the hotel. (Whittington.)

The Ambassador's flowered pergola walkways and cactus gardens were strategically situated among the bungalows that were advertised in 1929 as "outside rooms with bath as low as $5 per day." (CHS.)

The Cocoanut Grove Nightclub and Restaurant in the Ambassador Hotel was decorated in a Moroccan theme with fake palm trees and stuffed monkeys. It was extremely popular with moviemakers and film stars. All of the big band names played in the Grove, and Bing Crosby, Frank Sinatra, and Merv Griffin appeared there early in their careers. The Ambassador and the Grove made Wilshire a nighttime destination. (CHS.)

Besides Cocoanut Grove, the Ambassador provided several formal, smaller restaurants for its patrons. (Examiner.)

This aerial view looking north, taken in 1940, shows the Ambassador Hotel and grounds in the lower center. The Gaylord Hotel and Chapman Park Hotel are seen directly across Wilshire. (Whittington.)

The Gaylord Hotel and Apartments, located at 3355 Wilshire Boulevard at Kenmore, stood directly north of the Ambassador Hotel. Named after H. Gaylord Wilshire, it opened in 1924 as the "grande dame" of LA apartment hotels. It was built by Lilly and Fletcher and designed by Walker and Eisen. It included 13 stories, each with 33 suites. The lobby had terrazzo floors, travertine walls, iron chandeliers, and Persian rugs. The elevators had heavily carved walnut frames and walnut walls. An ivy-covered loggia and a walled garden were other features of the building. It was completely refurbished in 1977. (Whittington.)

The Chapman Park Hotel, located at 615 South Alexandria Street and 3401 Wilshire Boulevard, was a rambling Spanish-style building that served as the Olympic village for female athletes competing in the 1932 Olympic Games. It was then expanded with gardens and bungalows onto the site of the original Brown Derby restaurant. It was replaced by a 34-story Equitable Plaza office building that was erected in 1969. (CHS.)

A 1947 view of Wilshire Boulevard, east of Normandie Avenue, shows the Brown Derby restaurant, Gaylord Hotel and Mona Lisa Restaurant on the left and the entrance to the Ambassador on the right. (Whittington.)

The Beverly-Wilshire Apartment-Hotel, at 9500 Wilshire Boulevard and Rodeo Drive, was built by Walter G. McCarty at a cost of $4 million and opened on New Year's Eve in 1927. Photographed above in 1939, the nine-story, 352-room hotel was designed by Walker and Eisen in Beaux-Arts style. It included Southern California Classical and Churrigueresque details of engaged columns, balustrades, arcades, and a central tower, with extensive gardens behind the main building. Chandeliered dining rooms and ballrooms, and a marble lobby (seen below) were features that attracted exclusive clientele. The hotel underwent many renovations and changes to its original design, beginning with new owner Arnold Kirkeby in 1945, who added resort features such as a membership pool and spa, tennis courts, and the Copa Club. In 1961, Hernando Courtright, former general manager of the Beverly Hills Hotel, assumed control and revamped the traditional Oak Room into Hernando's Hideaway. In 1971, Courtright added a 14-story new wing with a grand ballroom that was designed by Welton Becket. (LAPL.)

This is the Beverly Hilton Hotel, located at 9876 Wilshire Boulevard. It was designed by Welton Becket and built in 1955 at the western boundary of Beverly Hills as the flagship hotel of Conrad Hilton's chain. The Hilton's International Ballroom was the city's largest and could accommodate 1,500 diners. It and the rooftop L'Escoffier restaurant became the home of many Hollywood society fundraisers and award shows. The Hilton served as the Kennedy Western White House in the early 1960s and hosted Pres. Lyndon Johnson. Below is a view of the hotel pool. (Whittington.)

Five

HOLLYWOOD

Hollywood evolved from a rural agricultural area in the late 19th century into a small resort town. Good weather and ocean views attracted people to this area, which is about six miles northwest of downtown Los Angeles. Harvey and Daeida Wilcox purchased a large tract near the Cahuenga Pass in 1886 and are credited with providing the name Hollywood to their subdivided property. By this time the railroads had connected Los Angeles with the rest of the United States, and well-off people from the East and the Midwest bought into the subdivision for winter or year-round homes. Hollywood was incorporated as a town in 1903. Because of the need for a water supply the municipality voted in 1910 to become part of the City of Los Angeles. In the early 20th century, Pacific Electric Railway trolleys connected Hollywood to the downtown business and cultural center of Los Angeles.

A number of early Hollywood hotels were either owned or managed by women, because hotel management was an area of employment open to women of means. Through the years, not only did Hollywood hotels serve as lodging places, but also their cafés, restaurants, and clubs with bandstand orchestras provided places where local residents, business people, tourists, and celebrities went for entertainment. During the 1920s, a period of major growth in Hollywood due to the rapidly expanding film industry, hotels hosted local cultural events, including art salons, society dinners, and film-industry events such as the Academy Awards. Hollywood hotels also served as headquarters for various local and national professional organizations that reflected new cultural and business developments in Southern California, including the new transportation field of aviation in the late 1920s and 1930s. Hotels, through the people and activities they hosted, have made a significant contribution to the national and international image of Hollywood as a place and as a lifestyle.

Sackett family members, seen here in 1898, are standing in front of the Sackett Hotel, framed by the post office and hardware store. Horace David Sackett and Ellen Sackett built the hotel in 1888 at Prospect (Hollywood Boulevard) and Cahuenga, an intersection that became an early Hollywood commercial center. In 1926, Ellen Sackett, then 78, attended a meeting of Hollywood pioneers as Hollywood's first hotelkeeper. Her daughter, Mary Sackett, who served as the first postmistress of the Hollywood post office located at the hotel, was also in attendance. Another Hollywood pioneer associated with the hotel was Dr. Edwin O. Palmer. Upon his arrival in California, he rented a room and an office for a medical practice in the hotel. Decades later, he purchased the hotel after he became a banker. He replaced the three-story Victorian wooden hotel with a two-story building that was enlarged in 1931 into the four-story Art Deco Creque Building at 6400–6408 Hollywood Boulevard that is still on the site. (LAPL.)

This photograph from the early 1900s shows the Six Mile House Hotel. In 1904, a newly formed city government of Hollywood closed down Casa Cahuenga restaurant at Sunset and Gower when the proprietor, J. W. Jeals, was fined for selling liquor in violation of a new Hollywood liquor ordinance. On October 27, 1911, William and David Horsley converted the Blondeau tavern on this site, informally known as the Six Mile House because of its distance from downtown Los Angeles, to the first Hollywood motion picture studio where several single-reel films were produced weekly until 1912. Various picture studios used the location until 1935, when Columbia Broadcasting purchased it. In 1940, a bronze memorial was placed on the site to commemorate it as the birthplace of the Hollywood film industry. (LAPL.)

The Glen Holly Hotel north of Prospect Avenue (Hollywood Boulevard) at Ivar and Yucca opened in 1900. The original proprietor, real estate developer Charles M. Pierce, operated a tallyho horse-drawn carriage that met tourists at the trolley from downtown Los Angeles to provide day tours of the Hollywood vicinity, including lunch at Glen Holly Hotel. In September 1901, 18 months after the opening of the Hollywood branch of the Los Angeles-Pacific Railroad, Los Angeles ex-Mayor Eaton and Councilmen Bowen and Walker attended a hotel banquet where the question of annexation to Los Angeles was discussed. The Glen Holly Hotel continued to be a lunch stop on sightseeing excursions of the Los Angeles Pacific Balloon Route from downtown, which Pierce took over as manager in 1904. D. L. Allen later took over management of the Glen Holly Tavern. Allen wanted to redevelop the hotel into a country-style resort to rival others in California, serving a cuisine of healthy vegetables raised on the site, and featuring amusements, including a billiard hall, bowling alley, and livery service. (CHS.)

In 1912, members of a nearby motion picture company assisted Mountain View Inn manager Mrs. Benjamin Fowler in evacuating all 50 guests when a chimney fire engulfed the hotel. The rebuilt hotel at 5956 Hollywood Boulevard, advertising such amenities as outdoor rooms, steam heat, switchboard services, and reasonable rates, was sold in 1924 to L. Rubin, a furrier in Utica, New York. In 1934, the Hollywood Chess Club located headquarters there. (LAPL.)

This 1916 photograph shows Lookout Mountain Hotel, built in 1910, twelve miles from downtown when it was advertised as a luxurious Southern California mountain resort with views of the ocean, mountains, valleys, and cities. It could be reached from Los Angeles by taking the Los Angeles Pacific and Laurel Canyon car to the end of the line, then by auto stage to the hotel. The hotel was destroyed in 1918 by a brush fire and was later developed as residential lots. (LAPL.)

This 1903 view shows Hollywood Hotel (Hotel Hollywood until the 1920s). A 1902 real estate advertisement for Hollywood highlighted the recent sale of a large block of land to George Hoover, president of the Bank of Hollywood and an investor in the Los Angeles Pacific Boulevard and Development Company, along with Harrison Gray Otis and developer H. J. Whitley, for the purpose of building a hotel to be named Hotel Hollywood. (LAPL.)

At the time the Hollywood Hotel was built, potential homebuyers arrived by electric car from Los Angeles. The hotel was promoted as a country resort hotel with modern conveniences and a first-class tourist and family hotel. Ms. Anderson and Ms. Stewart, who previously ran a family hotel at 1023 Bonnie Brae Street, operated it. (CHS.)

This photograph shows the expanded four-story Hollywood Hotel (1905–1910). At a formal banquet for 300 people that was held to mark the first hotel expansion in 1905, an early hotel guest spoke about views of barley fields from hotel windows when it first opened. The hotel hosted events, such as an annual Thanksgiving Day tennis tournament inaugurated in 1909, that established it as a social center. (CHS.)

This view of Hollywood in 1907 shows Hollywood Hotel on the left. The hotel was named in a court case involving the proprietor and Philo Beveridge, the governor's son and a prominent businessman, charged with serving wine to highway commissioners at a dinner, in violation of the city ordinance that prohibited the sale of alcohol. Ethel Barrymore stayed in the hotel when she performed at the Mason Theater in Los Angeles. (LAPL.)

This is a 1912 view of the Hollywood Hotel, the year it closed for a day as a result of a management dispute. The 200 guests were moved to the newly opened Hotel Beverly in Beverly Hills, owned and operated by Mrs. Anderson and her son. Mrs. Anderson, who had been the proprietor of Hollywood Hotel since it opened and had built up a fashionable clientele, left due to a disagreement with the new owner, Mira Hershey. (LAPL.)

In 1922, hotel owner Mira Hershey was involved in another dispute, a legal action by George Krom, manager of Hollywood Hotel since 1912, for alleged breach of a contract that was to allow him to purchase the hotel. The hotel was demolished in August 1956, so the site could be used for a First Federal Savings and Loan Association of Hollywood building. In 2008, it is the site of the Hollywood and Highland Kodak Theatre entertainment complex. (CHS.)

This 1927 photograph shows the pool area of the Spanish-style Garden of Allah Hotel and Villas at 8152 Sunset Boulevard. The hotel was developed as an extension of a mansion at 8080 Sunset Boulevard, built in 1919 by Russian-born Broadway actress, Alla Nazimova. Nazimova made her first silent film in 1916 and as Metro actress eventually became wealthy enough that she wrote and produced her own films. In 1927, she added 25 villas around the mansion, and the complex became known as the Garden of Allah. The name might be based on the 1905 novel by Robert Hichens, titled *Garden of Allah*, which was made into two silent films and a 1936 sound film starring Marlene Dietrich. The hotel attracted famous actors and writers, and was known for Nazimova's private parties, until her death in 1945. The Garden of Allah was demolished in 1959. It was developed into a small strip mall. (LAPL.)

This 1920s view of Hollywood Boulevard and the Hollywood area shows the Hotel Regent in the lower right at 6162 Hollywood Boulevard. Christie Realty Corporation, operated by Al and Charles Christie, built the hotel in 1925 for an estimated $500,000. It was on this site, when it was still an orange grove, that Nestor Company, of which Al Christie was manager and comedy director, did the first motion pictures shot in Hollywood. (LAPL.)

This pre–World War II view of Hollywood Boulevard shows an earlier Christie Brothers venture, the Hotel Christie, at McCadden Place and Hollywood Boulevard, as well as the Security First National Bank and tower and the sign for the Hotel Hollywood. In 1922, a new addition to the Hotel Christie, to be designed by architect Arthur Kelly, was announced. The hotel's Greenwich Village Café was a popular gathering spot for film industry people in the 1920s. (CHS.)

Above is a 1924 view of Garden Court Apartments and Hotel at 7021 Hollywood Boulevard. It shows the four-story courtyard residential hotel, designed by architect and developer Frank Meline in Beaux-Arts style and opened in 1919. Through the 1940s it was a glamorous address for film celebrities, including Mack Sennett, Lillian Gish, Rudolph Valentino, and John Barrymore. The Screen Actors Guild leased the building for a while and the structure was declared monument number 243 by Los Angeles City Council in 1981. It was, nevertheless, demolished in the early 1980s, and a decade passed before for the Hollywood Galaxy mall and Hollywood Entertainment Museum were built on the site. Pictured below in the 1930s is the Hotel Rector at Hollywood and Western. Built in the 1920s, the Rector provided rooms for stage and film actors and advertised daily rates at $1.50 to $2. (LAPL.)

The 1930s photograph of Hollywood and Western above shows the five-story steel frame, concrete and brick St. Francis Apartment-Hotel, at 5533 Hollywood Boulevard. It was purchased in 1928 by Hollywood Securities Corporation for $850,000. At the time, the Hollywood-Western District, bounded by Hollywood, Western, Franklin, and Sunset was projected to see new development near the hotel, such as executive and casting-bureau offices. Advertisements for St. Francis Hotel in 1950s listed rooms going for $2.50 a day. The photograph below from 1951 shows a view of Hollywood Boulevard looking west from Western Avenue with St. Francis Hotel on the right. In 2001 the Montreal-based hoteliers Urs Jakob and Suzanne Tremblay purchased the St. Francis and it is now the Gershwin Hotel/Hostel. Note the Pasadena-bound Pacific Electric streetcar on the tracks in the middle of Hollywood Boulevard. (LAPL and CHS.)

St. Moritz Hotel at 5849 Sunset Boulevard is on the right in this 1979 photograph. The hotel is located across the street from the former Warner Brothers Studio, which is now KTTV-Channel 5 and KMPC radio station. A 1939 advertisement promoted a room rental rate in the hotel at $7 weekly and compared it to a similar advertisement for the Christie Hotel, where the rooms were $35 weekly (LAPL.)

In 1941, the Guardian Arms Hotel and Apartments at 5217 Hollywood Boulevard advertised weekly rates from $35 to $85 in the heart of Hollywood. The building featured a small basement theater and was a rival to the Hollywood Hotel as a film star destination. A reception was held in 1958 for the renovation and renaming of the Guardian into Hollywood Hotel and Apartments. Today it is New Hollywood Apartments, located in the heart of East Hollywood. (LAPL.)

This 1951 photograph shows Chateau Elysée at 5930 Franklin Avenue. The seven-story steel and concrete hotel was built in 1929 by Eleanor Ince, widow of silent film producer Thomas H. Ince. Chateau Elysée was mentioned in *Los Angeles Times* society columns into the 1940s. Eleanor's son, 23-year-old film producer Richard Ince, died in 1938 after an accident in the 200-mile Pacific Coast motorcycle championship race at the Oakland Speedway, leaving behind his young wife of a few months whom he had married at the hotel. In 1951, owners Mr. and Mrs. G. E. Kinsey sold the hotel for $1 million and it was renamed the Fifield Manor Apartment Hotel after hotel board president Mrs. Fifield. It became a retirement hotel-apartment home that included lodging, food, medical care, hospitalization, and burial. In 1973, the Church of Scientology took over the hotel as part of the Celebrity Centre International, and it is now called Manor Hotel. (LAPL.)

The upper photograph shows the lobby of the Knickerbocker Hotel at 1714 North Ivar Avenue. Designed in Renaissance Revival Beaux-Arts style, the 300-room hotel catered to people arriving by train from the East Coast to work in theater and film. It was a popular social center; the managing director, A. O. Berghoff, brought in celebrities for the weekly Thursday Twilight Soirees hosted in the Cortile Lido. In 1934, well-known aviator Wiley Post stayed here for several days after flying from Oklahoma into Union Air Terminal in Burbank. The hotel, seen below in 1949, survived the Depression along with a number of hotels that were built in the 1920s in Los Angeles, though ownership changed hands over time. (LAPL.)

In 1955, Knickerbocker Hotel owner Ada McEntee sold it to Herman B. Sarno Associates, who rejuvenated the hotel and added a pool. The 1956 photograph above shows a televised opening ceremony for the improved hotel, broadcast on television station KRCA (4) and emceed by jet pilot Tom Frandsen. In 1963, a subsidiary of the Methodist Church purchased the Knickerbocker to operate as a hotel for permanent and transient guests, and in 1970 Standard Motels of Fresno purchased it from bankruptcy receivership. In 1972, Goldrich, Kest, Hirsch and Stern purchased the hotel and converted it to the Knickerbocker Apartments for senior citizens. Architects Brent, Goldman, Robbins, and Bown redesigned the building, retaining plaques in rooms dedicated to the film stars who previously stayed in the hotel. The photograph below shows Knickerbocker with the Capitol Records Building on the left in the 1960s. (Examiner and LAPL)

The 1930s aerial photograph above shows Hotel Roosevelt in mid-foreground, with the Hotel Christie a few blocks away. The Hotel Holding Company of Hollywood with president Joseph M. Schenck, and associates C.E. Toberman, Sid Grauman, Joseph Loeb, Louis B. Mayer, Marcus Loew, and others built the Roosevelt. In 1929, the first Academy Awards Ceremony was held here, and it was home to the Academy of Motion Picture Arts and Sciences from 1927 to 1935. The Roosevelt, shown below in the 1930s, was nationally famous in 1936 when the Hollywood Chamber of Commerce held a luncheon before the four-day air-racing program in Los Angeles. The event included well-known women aviators, such as Amelia Earhart, Ruth Elder, Laura Engalls, and Ruth Chatterton, and the president of the national air races, Carl Squier. (LAPL.)

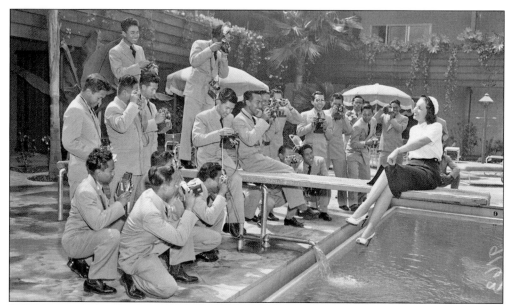

Indonesia Air cadets are shown at the Hollywood Roosevelt Hotel in 1951. In a ceremony to mark a 1950 hotel expansion, airline hostesses added containers of water from oceans around the world to the new swimming pool, and Esther Williams was invited to test the heated waters. Illinois Wesleyan University purchased the Roosevelt from Thomas Hull and his sister, Sally Crofwell, in the mid-1950s. (Examiner.)

This 1945 photograph shows the Art Deco Cinegrill in the Roosevelt, a combination grill, cocktail lounge and coffee shop designed by Maurice Trapet and featuring murals on the history of the film industry. The Cinegrill had the first structural glass front in a hotel in Southern California. Ernest Hemingway, Salvador Dali and other writers and artists were said to have socialized there. It also provided musical entertainment to the public. (LAPL.)

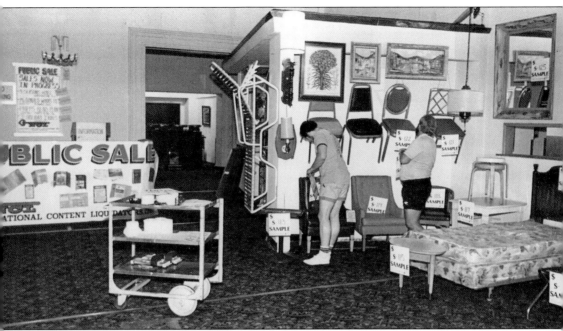

Taken in August 1984, this photograph shows furnishings that liquidators offered for sale during the 1950s' restoration of the Hollywood Roosevelt to its original Art Deco design. Workers spent several weeks pricing contents for sale, using wholesale catalogues and other reference works. During the mid-1980s, the hotel boom in Los Angeles resulted in traditional entrepreneurial hotel owners being bought out by hotel chain operators and investors. Hollywood Roosevelt was sold to several investment companies and underwent a $40-million renovation in 1985 employing a firm that worked on the original building, A. T. Heinsbergen and Company. Before the hotel closed for renovations in 1984, occupancy had gone down to five percent and graffiti adorned the walls. The swimming pool was in the news in the late 1980s when the David Hockney mural on the bottom of the pool that was part of the renovation project ran afoul of a state law that prohibited public pools from having designs shaped like swimmers, but the pool survived politics. The most recent hotel renovation was in 2005. (LAPL.)

This undated photograph shows Vine Street looking north towards Hollywood Boulevard from Sunset Boulevard, with the Plaza sign in the background. The Hollywood Plaza Hotel, designed by Walker and Eisen, was built at 1633-37 North Vine Street in 1924, at the same time that the Los Angeles Public Library at Fifth and Grand was under construction. The Hollywood Plaza Hotel opened on October 15, 1925 on a site that was previously the residence of Jacob Stern. The 10-story, T-shaped Hollywood Plaza had two enclosed garden plazas, which served as the inspiration for the hotel's name. Joseph Stern owned the hotel. For 99 years, he leased it to the Vine Street Hotel and Investment Company, headed by Harold Stern. The original reinforced concrete building with ornamental plaster and stone cost $1 million. (LAPL.)

Hollywood Plaza Hotel, shown here in 1927, was one of several hotels in Hollywood that accommodated executives and entertainers in the growing film and radio broadcasting industries. The hotel had 198 apartment-style rooms with tiled baths and a Spanish-style lobby. It featured lavish drapery by Los Angeles Drapery Company and furniture by Los Angeles Roberti Brothers, designed by George Benedict. The ladies room was said to be a replica of Marie Antoinette's boudoir at Fontainebleau. Klemtner's Café opened to the public on October 15, 1925, with blue-plate service on imported china, lavishly upholstered cathedral booths, a counter with revolving chairs, and tables for up to 150 guests for meals and afternoon teas. In 1937, Ernest Hemingway checked into the Plaza on his first visit to Hollywood, when Robert Benchley threw him a party at Garden of Allah. In 1926, the new Hollywood Aero Club opened headquarters in the plaza, and in 1927 it displayed here a model of a new vacuum-propelled dirigible aircraft. (LAPL.)

This 1945 view from Selma north towards Vine shows Studio Theater, Plaza Hotel, and Broadway Hollywood. The Taft and the Brown Derby are visible across the street. Walker and Eisen designed the Taft Building, where prospective entertainers found agents. The duo also designed the Plaza Hotel. Control of Hollywood Plaza had been assumed by Hull Hotels in 1936 and leased from the Eugene Stern estate. Other local hotels controlled by Hull were Hollywood Roosevelt and the Mayfair on Seventh Street in Los Angeles. Thomas Hull, formerly a Colorado mining engineer, was an aviator in the 113th Aerial Squadron in World War I. The hotel lease transferred in 1939 to Joseph Drown and in 1951 to Lawrence Lee, who opened a renovated hotel with a new coffee shop and lounge in 1952. The following year, he added an L-shaped pool. (LAPL.)

The new $125,000 Cinnabar restaurant at the Hollywood Plaza, seen here in an undated photograph, had a gala opening in December 1936 that was attended by film stars. Designated directors' and writers' corners were unveiled along with murals depicting film history. Hotel manager Ivan Stauffer announced he had hired an internationally known chef to provide cuisine to meet the sophisticated whims of the entertainment set. (LAPL.)

This 1937 photograph shows It Café at the Hollywood Plaza Hotel, opened by Clara Bow. Al Jolson celebrated here after he broadcasted the premiere of his new radio show at Vine Street Theater. Phil Selznick took over the Café in 1939 and closed it in 1943. A 1962 *Los Angeles Times* article credited restaurant manager Paul Grubb with creating the Cesar salad for the actor Cesar Romero. (LAPL.)

DISCOVER THOUSANDS OF LOCAL HISTORY BOOKS FEATURING MILLIONS OF VINTAGE IMAGES

Arcadia Publishing, the leading local history publisher in the United States, is committed to making history accessible and meaningful through publishing books that celebrate and preserve the heritage of America's people and places.

Find more books like this at
www.arcadiapublishing.com

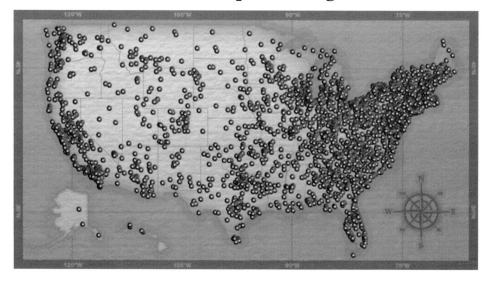

Search for your hometown history, your old stomping grounds, and even your favorite sports team.